CLASSICAL CHART HITS

GOLD

Published by:
Music Sales Limited,
8/9 Frith Street, London W1D 3JB, England.

Exclusive Distributors:
Music Sales Limited,
Distribution Centre, Newmarket Road, Bury St. Edmunds, Suffolk IP33 3YB, England.
Music Sales Corporation,
257 Park Avenue South, New York, NY10010, United States of America.
Music Sales Pty Limited,
120 Rothschild Avenue, Rosebery, NSW 2018, Australia.

Order No. AM976316
ISBN 0-7119-9803-5
This book © Copyright 2003 by Wise Publications.

Printed in the United Kingdom.

Your Guarantee of Quality:
As publishers, we strive to produce every book to the highest commercial standards.
The music has been carefully designed to minimise awkward page turns
and to make playing from it a real pleasure.
Particular care has been given to specifying acid-free, neutral-sized
paper made from pulps which have not been elemental chlorine bleached.
This pulp is from farmed sustainable forests and was produced
with special regard for the environment.
Throughout, the printing and binding have been planned to ensure a sturdy,
attractive publication which should give years of enjoyment.
If your copy fails to meet our high standards, please inform us and we will gladly replace it.

www.musicsales.com

WISE PUBLICATIONS
part of the Music Sales Group

London/New York/Paris/Sydney/Copenhagen/Berlin/Madrid/Tokyo

1812 Overture

(Finale)

Composed by Pyotr Ilyich Tchaikovsky

Allegro vivace

Adagio for Strings

featured in 'Platoon'

Composed by Samuel Barber

Moderato adagio (very slowly)

(with increasing intensity)

Canon in D major

Composed by Johann Pachelbel

13

15

Casta Diva

from Norma

Composed by Vincenzo Bellini
Arranged by Simon Lesley

Andante sostenuto ($\quad$. = 50)

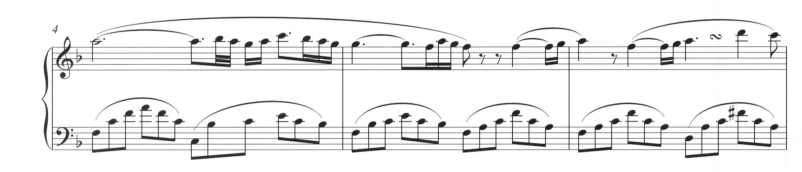

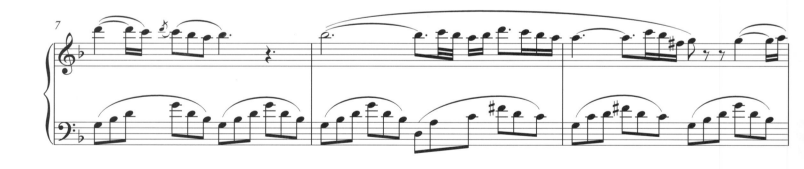

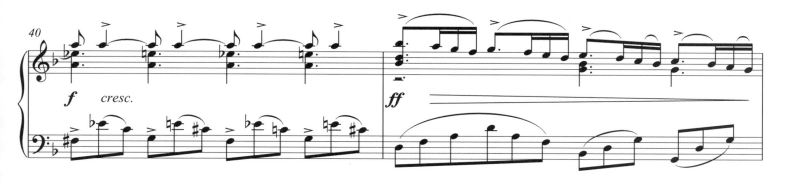

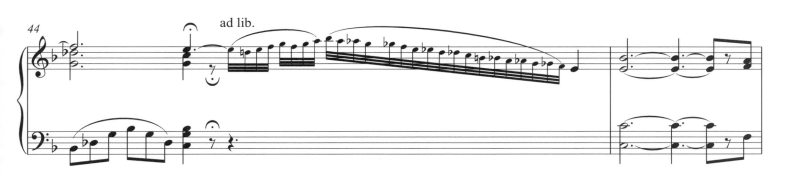

Chorus of the Hebrew Slaves (Va Pensiero)

from Nabucco

Composed by Giuseppe Verdi

Concerto for Clarinet and Orchestra in A major, K622

(Adagio)

Composed by Wolfgang Amadeus Mozart

Concerto for Two Violins in D minor

(2nd Movement: Largo ma non troppo)

Composed by Johann Sebastian Bach
Arranged by Jerry Lanning

Concerto for Violoncello and Orchestra
in E minor, Op.85

(1st Movement: Adagio)

Composed by Sir Edward Elgar

Dance of the Reed Flutes

from The Nutcracker

Composed by Pyotr Ilyich Tchaikovsky

Flower Duet

from Lakmé

Composed by Leo Delibes
Arranged by Simon Lesley

Delicately (♪ = 112)

very little pedal

Hallelujah Chorus

from Messiah

Composed by George Frideric Handel

Jupiter, the Bringer of Jollity

from The Planets, Op.32

Composed by Gustav Holst
Arranged by Jerry Lanning

Allegro giocoso ♩ = 120

La Ci Darem La Mano

from Don Giovanni

Composed by Wolfgang Amadeus Mozart
Arranged by Jack Long

Lacrymosa

from Requiem in D minor, K626

Composed by Wolfgang Amadeus Mozart

Nessun Dorma

from Turandot

Composed by Giacomo Puccini

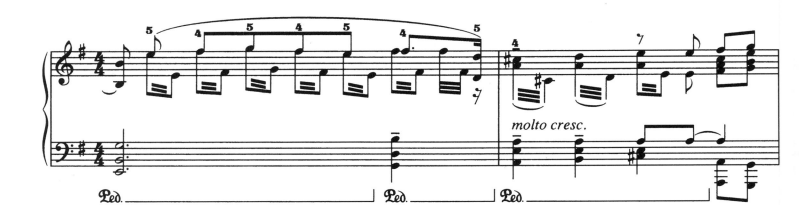

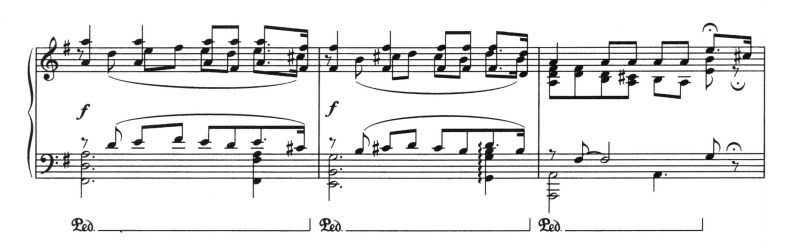

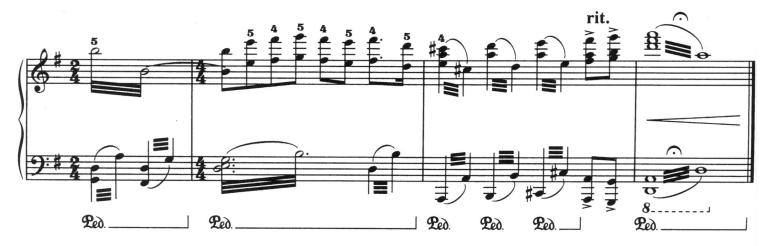

The Toreador Song

from Carmen

Composed by Georges Bizet

Allegro molto moderato

Piano Concerto No.1 in B♭ minor, Op.23
(Opening)

Composed by Pyotr Ilyich Tchaikovsky

Allegro non troppo

Piano Sonata No.23 in F minor

(2nd Movement: Andante con moto)

Composed by Ludwig van Beethoven

Andante con moto

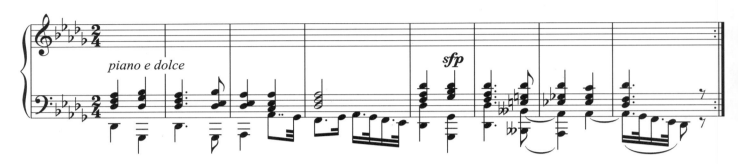

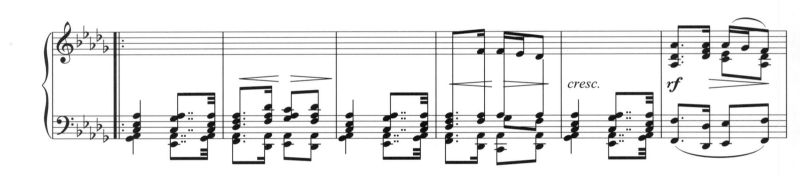

The Ride of the Valkyries

featured in 'Apocalypse Now'

Composed by Richard Wagner
Arranged by Jerry Lanning

Spring

(1st Movement: Allegro)
from Violin Concerto in E major 'The Four Seasons'

Composed by Antonio Vivaldi

Symphony No.5 in C minor, Op.67

(Theme)

Composed by Ludwig van Beethoven
Arranged by Jack Long

Allegro con brio (♩ = 108)

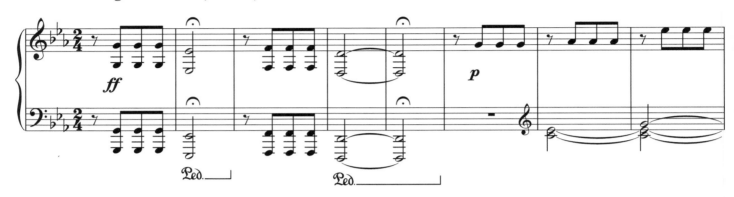

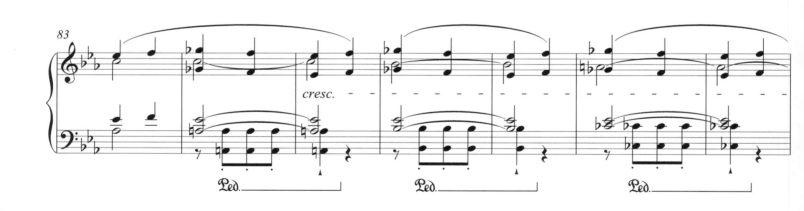

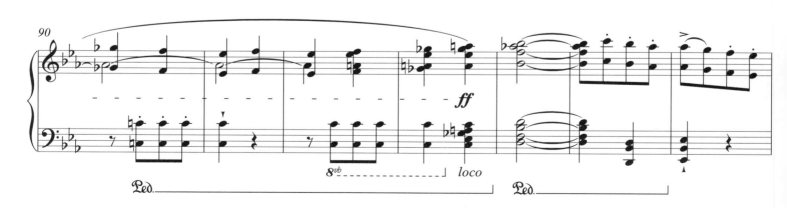

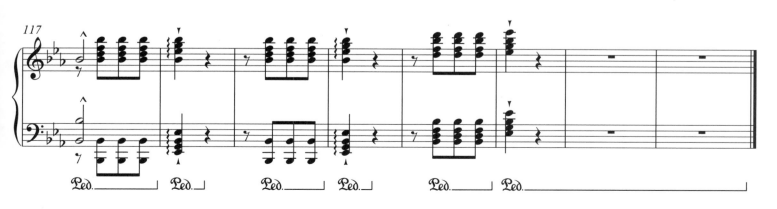

Symphony No.5 in C♯ minor

(4th Movement)
featured in 'Death in Venice'

Composed by Gustav Mahler

Symphony No.9 'Choral'

(2nd Movement: Molto vivace)

Composed by Ludwig van Beethoven
Arranged by Jack Long

Waltz from The Sleeping Beauty

Composed by Pyotr Ilyich Tchaikovsky
Arranged by Jerry Lanning

Zadok the Priest

(Coronation Anthem)

Composed by George Frideric Handel

Andante maestoso